DEAR
OUTSIDERS

AKRON SERIES IN POETRY

AKRON SERIES IN POETRY

Mary Biddinger, Editor

Titles published since 2014.
For a complete listing of titles published in the series,
go to www.uakron.edu/uapress/poetry

DEAR
OUTSIDERS

Jenny Sadre-Orafai

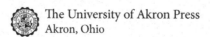

The University of Akron Press
Akron, Ohio

ISBN: 978-1-62922-238-7 (paper)
ISBN: 978-1-62922-239-4 (ePDF)
ISBN: 978-1-62922-240-0 (ePub)

LIBRARY OF CONGRESS CATALOGING-IN-PUBLICATION DATA
Names: Sadre-Orafai, Jenny, author.
Title: Dear outsiders / Jenny Sadre-Orafai.
Description: First edition. | Akron, Ohio : The University of Akron Press, 2023. | Series:
  Akron series in poetry
Identifiers: LCCN 2022052878 (print) | LCCN 2022052879 (ebook) | ISBN 9781629222387
  (paperback) | ISBN 9781629222394 (pdf) | ISBN 9781629222400 (epub)
Subjects: LCGFT: Poetry.
Classification: LCC PS3619.A3533 D43 2023 (print) | LCC PS3619.A3533 (ebook) |
  DDC 811/.6—dc23/eng/20221108
LC record available at https://lccn.loc.gov/2022052878
LC ebook record available at https://lccn.loc.gov/2022052879

∞ The paper used in this publication meets the minimum requirements of ANSI/NISO
z39.48–1992 (Permanence of Paper).

Cover image: *Friend Ends With an End*, by Cristina Daura. Cover design by Amy Freels.

Dear Outsiders was designed and typeset in Minion with Helvetica titles by Amy Freels and
printed on sixty-pound natural and bound by Baker & Taylor Publisher Services of Ashland,
Ohio.

Produced in conjunction with the University
of Akron Affordable Learning Initiative.
More information is available at
www.uakron.edu/affordablelearning/

for LM and for my students

Contents

◇

There was no space for a continuous forest
no space for an infinite sea
no matter how endless the search.

—Garous Abdolmalekian

Topographies

An egret with a fish speared on his beak.
Not your hands twisting out the wet from a shirt.

Steam from a shower that belongs to our mother.
Not a fire scrubbing us all.

A branch leaning too hard on a fence.
Not a mail carrier reaching for letters we write our parents.

Balancing on one leg, our hands over our heads at the end of the water.
Not a broken flag in our neighbor's yard.

Our mother's body.
Not our mother's body.

Our father's body.
Not our father's body.

A grief bleating at our shores.
A landscape breaking.

Beginnings of Nature

Our parents decide. Land. Water. We memorize the legend, the map. Our parents choose water, grip us in fish traps. Every day is a riding wave. One inch is eleven and a half miles. Always on top of the water until you're not. Safe as long as you stay. We don't harbor agitators. They're sunk before they're old enough to swim away. We don't open our box, offer throw rings. Our parents tell us that all the water in the world has been here forever, that the world will never make new water—no matter how many mouths it has. Don't bother trying to ask in babysong.

When We Are So Young

We watch nameless couples walk near the water. Our parents teach us what legs mean, what synchronized means—mirrors. We cast futures on them before we can even talk whole words into needs. We follow down the shore until they are threads. How many pictures have we been in without knowing? The tourists call themselves visitors. We're supposed to call them guests. It's a trap. We never watch after our parents. We aren't allowed to assign them lives they can't live. We don't pull the thread, the net, the warning into our chests.

Fortune Fish

We win a red cellophane fish—his body like antique onionskin. The paper envelope he's kept in must be as old as our parents. The envelope tells us to hold him in one palm and be very still. *You are so excited.* The Ferris wheel's light catches on his tail. We take him out to the water, let him swell with the bigger fish. We pick up two shells and hold them over both our ears. The waves slap our house inside our heads. This is where we were born, we say to the fish camp. Everyone on the boardwalk claps when the scenes get shuffled—the sun goes down and the fireworks cruise comes out from behind the curtain.

Occupation Interview

A quiz at school interviews us, tells us who we'll be when we grow up. We both get astronaut. And when we go so far out in the water, we're sure that one day a real and willing astronaut will land in our arms and teach us gravity and floating. We catch ourselves with our chins in the air, the water choppy and lapped against our necks, looking out for a wilted parachute to land on the crest of our waves. And then we play the game where the ocean is our dress, and we slip anchors on our feet while we watch the lifeguards wheel out their wooden stands where they lord over.

Scale & Embodiment

We eat crackers as we walk on the pier. The terns follow us like we're new suns. At the end, a fisher has caught a stingray. People who aren't fishermen gawk around him, take pictures, ask questions. We bend away to look at a ship—a thumb on the ocean. We watch the birds watch us even though we're finished with the crackers. Birds follow food always. The glint of the birds' feathers in the silent wind and sun. The breathing ray, the length of its tail. The color of the boat that is so far away that maybe we wouldn't even be able to say for sure or something so brilliant it hurts.

Field Test

We stare at a house that looks more like a barn. How can it be this far away? We're sure if we look very hard, we will see what the people inside must be doing. It's the second of three visual field tests. We're given a hand buzzer for the last one and we have to focus on a dot while clicking the buzzer any time we see squiggled lines on the screen. One eye at a time. We pretend we're on a game show and that we only have right answers. Our father tells us when we are small and then when we are big *you have two ears and one mouth*. He never talks about how many eyes we have. What are we looking for? Why are we looking? A family eating oatmeal, folding socks into each other, reading in natural light, stirring simple soups into so small a house.

Glory Pact

Our mother promises us that this home can't burn. Fire won't flock, won't peel one sad shingle away, can't feed on these seagrass floors. You won't squint at the stop sign two-and-a-quarter miles from here and see grey puffs like sighs. Not this place that's never felt fire in its hearth. She tells us dolphins come here to give birth since there aren't too many sharks. Our home is a snake with pulled teeth.

Tragedy Lesson

Describe drown. We don't say it too loud when it happens. It's not for the hotel people, people who pay for symmetrical shells. They walk out so far that they can't tell which place is theirs on the way back. We're sure there's nothing that could keep them away anyway. Not the burns. Not even if we told all the jellies to wait outside their *do not disturb* doors. We know them by the color of their towels. Orange is the fanciest resort. Blue is the motel without water views. They line their balconies with them—flags to countries they'll never belong to. The body is rescued and buried because it didn't swim at 45 degrees to shore. There aren't long talks over dinners. We're so sorry and that's enough.

Singing School

Describe the trees. Cypress knees adjust to water, breathe under to keep from suffocating. We dive down watching for their inhale, their trick we tried to outlast again and again. We dream reels of blank, reams of nothing. We take deep breaths and grab at every rainbow on the horizon. We speak to manatees in a language we use for dolphins and they don't say anything back. We don't mind the mud that smells like dead eggs. We're convinced we can sense if other animals need rescue by their bark in movies. We bring the neighbor's brindled dog into the family room and play the animal parts to be sure the animals were really safe. Not that there was anything we could do.

Low Recitation

We open the maps like menus. Like we're ordering for the whole table. We rotate them on our desks. They sound like our parents with their newspapers in the mornings. We try to see different pictures, but the blue is flat kudzu, hushing the land's arteries. Name the world's seven continents. Name the world's five oceans. We think we see our mother's body shape there. Use your pointer finger to show me land. How many of you were born there? What is plateau? What is plain? Basin? Now use your pointer finger to show me ocean. How many of you were born right here? What is a current? Crest? What is undertow? That's right. This is the rip that sweeps bodies under and into her chest.

Lost & Found

You can tell who the locals are. Our eyes are closed. We've watched the ocean breathe our entire lives. Sometimes the wood storks ride the water and sometimes it's blank. It's not new. People who visit take shells, fractured to almost dust, back home. They hold their babies up in the morning to the water. They kick sand and step on our stuff. We know the ocean is more than something to look at. They carry miniature prizes in their hands—shell dust, a tooth, an aluminum drink top. We point out the prettiest shells and we live for when they pick it up and get clipped. They'll start stinking if they get them home. We have a store with clean and painted shells for people who aren't us to feel good about buying. We imagine they take the shells home in the store netting and tell people I caught these just like this. We don't filch. We don't take from our own pail.

Decoys

At night when the boats run engines, we race up the lighthouse stairs, shuttered, tourist trap. We get to the top, slouch to our knees, breathe so hard it tastes like blood. Our lungs are open clams. We stand up and straight, we take steps backwards away from each other without looking behind. We know the owl decoys are scaring no one. Other birds perch on their unmovable heads. We won't get hurt. Our mother makes us write down what we wear every day—a chart on the front door in case we're abducted. That's not the point. We can't turn the lights on after nine anywhere. The turtle babies will think we're the moon. We throw our light everywhere though. We say we'll guide the thumbs on the ocean home.

Someone Yelled Fire

Describe where you put the futures. Our parents say that we can tell the ocean all the dooms we see on the shore. Go out there and throw them off. They won't reach back here. They won't grab onto the barnacle belt. The terns, black skimmers, even the crows, aren't looking for what you've got to say. Just as the gulls shake out their feathers, dusty rugs, the people from the hotel are out on the beach. They're stunned cannonballs so surprised that this is where they ended up. The stingrays swoon, a crushing encore.

Heard Said

We leave them with their continental breakfasts they eat because it's free. We watch their lazy mouths drink orange juice and stare at the rain. They calculate how much money they've wasted. How much yoga they can't do on the beach. The hotel umbrellas look like they're laughing with us. We cross the bridge to the rougher water. No guards. We swim up to the ice cream dinghy. We follow the cherry on top from so far off. Our mother ate ice cream here when she was younger than us now. We sit on the edge, licking our cones until they're ate. Swimming back real slow, we always hear our mother—that eating anything and swimming is asking for a stomachache and you two were born here, don't come to me when you forget that swimming saves you.

Souvenirs for Locals

dirty clothes in a laundry bag the size of a sitting ten-year-old / orange sunglasses with GUARD on the arms / braided nylon flip flops / keys to electric cars / keys to houses on mountains / keys to fireproof safes / steel credit cards / a stuffed brown horse with a saddle stitched onto its body / a warped passport with no stamps / a bag of cash / a remote / two red plastic shovels / a yellow gold chain / an army survival manual

Anchor Bend

When we want to visit the starfish, we swim out. We aren't allowed when they're giving tours to hotel people. We know starfish have eyes even if we can't see them on their faces just like we know the vanishing island is real even though sometimes it disappears—the tides covering it up, lost and found. We feel what the other feels and if one of us swims too fast, the other's legs hurt and we both have to take a break. Sometimes we think one of us will dissolve.

Casting

During gym, we file along the edge of a sprawled parachute. We lift it high above our heads, see each other underneath the stained-glass dome. We don't know what we're supposed to learn. Don't fight the current. With her good arm, our teacher pitches fuzzed balls on top. We make swells, watch them jump into sweaty air. The balls are coffinships, good for nothing. You'll drift and you won't know where you are. We let go of our corner and it's a jelly suffocating an island.

Magic Slate

We watch ourselves blur. When she takes showers, we walk into the bathroom and up to the wicker mirror. We blow air out of our lips before we disappear. We see ourselves get covered up, steam coming for our eyes first and then we are gone. It's a game to see who will die first. Our mother never plays. But when we see a man in town who has cataracts in his right eye, a cloud that never goes away, we stop. We give our mother her showers back—we're a tide that's gone back in.

Half a Parade

You can't see where the water ends no matter what. We time how long we can last, how many miles, before looking it up. We bow, careful egrets, and say it's our pleasure to be in the presence of such a gown of water. We see our dad paint on the boardwalk on weekends. Girls on floats dance to music from a portable loudspeaker. The ocean's an animal head on a wall, and we can't see the body. We think it must be inside the wall and that it walks out at night when we sleep. What's a body really.

Stacks

Our father balanced rocks in a past life. He lived by a river he doesn't remember, and he tells us that this is why he came from the land and the mountains this life. He talks about tectonic plates, how mountains were formed, describes floating continents and what will happen when all the water in the world is disappeared. We saw a stack of pink roses on the beach once. It was early winter, and they were dozens. They belonged to us. Everything did in the cold. Not even the gulls wanted them. Without the water, we'd be without our mother. Without our father, we would lose the world under our knees. When you love the beach, you love it no matter what.

No Wake Zone

We go to neighborhood pools and our feet get sore and rough, red at the edges. Where is the salt, the smell, the slime, the sea stars immobile and magnified. Our eyes haze from chemicals and our bodies lean into each other, cinnamon sticks, walking up the steps, our feet slap against the wet cement. We can hear the pirate festival—out of towners captured every year for fun. Other parents tell us, no running. We see our falls—our heads opening up and the gulf rushing out.

True/False

How many tails are in this piece of the gulf? Whose idea was it to make so much water? What happens when water becomes a gas? How long can you hold your breath at the state fair? Who is the sun and who is the moon? How can a human have a mouth and so can water? Why do we make wishes on feathers? How do you flush saltwater out of an engine? If a vulture is gold, what is its meal? How long can we turn in circles before we lose our names? What is the probability of throwing two ones? What's the man's name who names the storms?

The Way Home

We know migration patterns of wet animals. One spring butterflies spot the quiet water and we swim close to see if they're still living. Our mother has reasons for their deaths and for their funerals. For why she only plays solitaire in the summer on her bed, making a bridge every time she shuffles. Only one wing per wave. A parade of failed butterflies lines the way home. We watch them string together on the way to school. Our science teacher doesn't have the answers. She tells us it's just too hot for all of us. There's not enough water to cool us back down.

Trauma Management

A man at the bait shop calls us family. His worms all nod, agree. We've seen him nodding off in his sagged chair. We've watched him pull up his invisible line when we walk by. What is there to see except for a fish trying to swim away from a line and then back into its life. How the waves can look choppy for a sun but calm for coral. We turn his voice off and recite the alphabet backwards. We count the wild horses on the boat.

Locals

People who aren't us think that the ocean is all blue but there are lines if you look hard. Water isn't easy to read. We say dolphins can stay underwater twenty minutes tops. We tell them that we bury our dead boats in container ships. We say the waves are clapping for you. We say there are reasons why we don't build our houses taller than our trees. We don't tell them that the town is taking the toll away. We only warn the small children about going out higher than their waists. We point out what they should take pictures of even though it's nothing. We go past the buoys, warnings floating, and the lifeguards don't say a thing. We aren't worth the trouble. We're a reflection swimming backward. We're crabs breaking the pot.

Divining

There will always be our mechanic and his swinging metal detector. He's not looking for anything as much as this has become the way his body moves now. We know some kids who dissect old belts and bury the gold parts. They hide between dunes, watching him dig, a child making a lopsided moat. There's nothing to do but wait until he's left holding the belt, broken. The ocean foam frames the pelicans and the violence in their dives again and again. Their good eyes take us in.

Boat Call

Blown Away / Argo / Cheers / Anchor Boy / Apparent Breeze / River Whisper / Mean Wind / Yesterday's Storm / Precious Drifter / Verdant Hope / Sober Nook / Knotty Obsession / Lake Tub / Good Legend / Second Key / Rogue Wave / Bay Dream / Due South / Aqua Life / Knot From Around Here / Wayward Sun / Second Tequila / The Pearl / Don't Panic

Affirmations

The algae ruin our shoes. Wild, we push our hands onto urchin and crab. Gulls don't want you touching their food. Somebody tell them their gullets aren't made for sea stars. Somebody tell everybody that sea stars aren't starfish. Somebody tell the starfish we're sorry for buying their bodies (starched like pressed clothes) from the store just because shells were gold, capital. Tell the store our house is a conch and they'll never have more than us. When you're rich like this, you never think about dying.

Because If Someone Heard Us

They would save us. The first boy our mother kissed owns a peacock farm and sometimes we go there and play with his daughter. On our way, there's a heap of blown tires collected on the side of the road. Someone with a truck that says *Fast Service* on the side will move it because it's an eyesore. Sometimes we go with our father to the art store where his hands gradually tug at the mini paints. He fans them in his hand, looking down at a warming full flush. The birds call, clean themselves in the dirt. Everyone hears and no one is on the verge of saving them.

Forgiveness Toll

Double red flags whip on a different beach. Across the bridge. Water is used against our parents' bodies. We aren't there. Forgive our feet. They move like breakers. One part of the lifeguard test is to rescue bricks from the bottom of a pool. They have to keep it above their heads and out of the water while they swim on their backs. Everyone passes this test. We've watched them. This is our dispatch. Rescue lights turn their heads around and around. They say our parents sank. They take forever to radio out to us.

One More Origin Story

She said the gulf spat her out and yes, we believed. Her fingers never wrinkled from water—a cormorant. Our mother swam past markers, past chartered boats, and never turned around for a crowd of applause. No guard radioed in her bright back. What else can we tell you but she's an orphan from an atmosphere we don't know. She saw the crawler crusher make this place. We take her fin, paddle out.

Land Stories

We hear the woods are an open palm. We hear *please bring playing cards*. There isn't much left to make a stream of. No water vein. We're told we like the black snakes. They eat the mice. Wear the bear bell hard, let them know you're coming. Their eyes aren't sharp. Don't shave your underarms. Turn all the lights off at night if you don't want moths beating themselves until they die, peppering your doorstep, softening your step down.

At Our Lessons We're Given a Map

The first cricket of spring sounds like a live wire. Water is the width of one hair, fine and light, almost a pencil mistake on the land. It's all seed and feed here. But if we focus hard, there's our father's face, a cliff. We can find a way to live there, pitch a house but not a home. Use your pointer finger to show me land. How many of you were born right here? Home has been constellated. Flung. Do you know where you are?

Factors Influencing Life

A fountain performs for the sun and we divide the spurts, one for them and two for us. Robins subtract the light. We sit with the backyard. Watertight. No one wants it. The bird bath is a bowl of resin, oak leaves in history. We see the shoulders of the sunrise, and we lock it out of the shed, wrap the mower in tarp. We draft a warranty stating we will always sleep with the dresses our mother made, her signature in the hems. We will always wake up to our father's paintings on our very own. We forfeit our inheritances if we forget. There was that time when our mother and father drowned, and we hid every letter of their names. We lived in a house on the edge of a dry bed.

Lessons for Waywards

And it was our mother with big water hair who first taught us to kiss our turned-up hems and how to play cards alone. We whisk and beat our dresses to death. We fossil them in the front yard's garden bed. We are so exhausted from hearing night flowers that we make up our own beds and then plant ourselves there until we can't make out our breathing. It was our father who said we are only meant to remember as much as we can. And now we are saying we won't remember the lessons or the front yards or what time when our mother was pulled, her hair big, an ocean in an ocean and how loud everything got when our father died for good too.

A Field, A Flood

We walk out here with our knees high. It's how everyone knows our parents chose water for us. We walk the packed land like walking against a cresting tide. They call it a march. We're beetles struggling on concrete sidewalks. They ask us: *where is the rest of the band, marchers?* They give us looks at the food store. We're fine around stairs and large fields. Our legs always synchronized. Which lesson is when we forget sand? How will history treat us and our stubborn knees? When will we not be hungry for our parents, for the shattering portraits under our feet?

Double-Face Mirror

Everyone says to snake poison down the throat when the roots shoot through the tub. Everyone. They say *trees that sway together stay together*. We haul water. All the water in the world is all the water there'll ever be. They say that they know how to read the mailbox even though the flag is broken. We get down in the bath and say this water has got to be the star and this root must be our mother, the good net. Her hair watching us, singing every song she knows.

In Our Awful Sweet Voice

Common spiders appear in our bedroom like shadows. We take a glass left behind for short drinks and press the rim against the walls. Sliding our lessons between the glass and the wall, we dial into the emergency radio. Then we carry their jumpy bodies, buttons come loose, out to day lilies. Everything goes back where it belongs except for us. The home draped on the beach. *Out came the rain and washed the shadows out.* This happens so many days. We start to silver.

Levels of Force

All the lamps we've had we've hugged too hard. At night, the shadow is our mother's waist and hips and skirt. The world will take back the water and wind if we can get our rooms just right. One of us stays in the house while the other pours water outside against the ribs of the house with drenched shoes that belonged to our mother. The one in the house says louder! Louder! Make it like we were born here! And then we rake through our braids and our armpits for salt and sand and come up empty.

Learning Weather

How many fogs we get in the summer is how many snows in the winter. How many cricket chirps make one degree? Home, we'd watch fish faint on the top of the water for rain. We'd see the fishers herd and strand them. Here, we read the leaves' glimmered turns like a game of solitaire. Who wins? The house. Nature always wipes us clean.

Dear Outsiders

Young boys here cut bad words and bad pictures into fall cover crops. Words like fuck and shit and damn. Pictures like penises and testicles. The fact that we can't read them since we're on the land means that they aren't meant for us, the wayward marchers. Their mothers and fathers look at the butchering they've done, and they're kept from fun and cars and formals that we won't go to either. And we're writing to say that you shouldn't be so loud when you walk if you want to blend in. Their pool lifeguards are soft and their sad whistles wilt on their necks when they sigh into them. If you want to say you were born here, lower your knees.

The Swap

birdfeeders / saws / cast iron pans / ammunition in boxes / guns / boiled peanuts / license plates / barbeque sauce / soft leather gloves / diabetic socks / cutting boards / camo vests / music records / drinking glasses / guitars / dogs on leashes / pocketknives / doorknobs / magnetic bracelets / dog bandannas / magnetic jar openers / peaches / statues of football players / paisley ties / standing dolls with crocheted skirts / ice cream cones / motor oil / headstones

Signs of Water

We're in town for muscadines when we hear a squeaky wheel. We drop our walk to look for what. The wheel sweeps the sun. Nearly synchronized, we look up. A seagull. A sand dollar beating on the sky. And we try to drain everything below the blue and replace it with a pushing tide. Blue on blue. We stand there and like that for so long. The gull is gone before we can tell it we're a scarecrow.

Pencils Down

After the barren days, everyone's out planting then deadheading. We
drop our rescue glass. Slices on the counter and on the floor. We don't
move our feet, and the spider climbs deep down into the tub's throat.
Feet planted, we bend over to pick up the broke glass and quietly slide
it in the trash. In goes an arm lifting out of water, waving. When the
shards fall, they become sea glass tumbling and our father saying *time
to go, only one more piece.* We plant live forever. We water the garden,
the house, a chipmunk who doesn't flinch when we water him too.

Healing Response

We've seen our parents whisper on their knees. Our father after showers. Our mother before traveling. It was private and they never showed us how to believe in anything but them. We knew they would save us from a riptide, from a drowning. And we had a dog who was so sick that she was always dying, and our saving was to feed her all her favorite foods and then tell the animal doctor to put her asleep. We didn't ask for her body back. What's left of what's dead. Her toys. Her hairs on the couch. More than we could stuff in our pockets.

The Start of the Thread

We were raised up by our mother's singing. She took the lead, the start of the thread, in every song and we let her. Her hands opened like she carried invisible plates to feed everyone. We were raised up by our father's paintings drying on the walls, turpentine hung in the windows and refused to leave. We don't push our mouths into singing since we lost her and when we found a tube of paint someone left behind, we squeezed it all out onto the sidewalk and let the sun eat it right up.

Here, in the Summer

We mistake the neighbor children for cats. Their mewls come out in the afternoon when they run into rusted sprinklers brave and clumsy. Their bodies aren't deliberate in the way ours are when we look for juniper in between their chairs that are sunny and too small for anyone but dolls. We hear their babies crying through the house walls. We put out milk before we understand what we aren't feeding. There are rivers of milk between their ribs.

Their Eyes Glassed & Curious

Our fence is brought down by a family of bear. A sleuth. A sloth. The open patch they left bends the fence back with the charge of their bodies. We imagine their paws rattling what was left of our border. We don't put it back up because we're lonely. We look toward the gap— rolled earth, train bed, mud lake. We leave water out. We manage. We think we can see them breathing through their noses against our scenes at night.

Making More of Ourselves

We cut the woods like a deck of cards. We make straight lines and don't leave rooms open for bears to seep into. One-lane roads no one can pass. We let owls crease at the corners, living gargoyles. We count to fifteen in our mouths and then here we come for all of the herbs nipping at our feet. We bottle and can. We stop every plant up. We wait for the crickets who only sing to mate, and we all have to hear it don't we. We all shoulder their desire to make more of themselves. Our ears pop and everything smells like soil.

Growing Our Own Doctor

Our mother is the first vow and the last vow. We say them both. A woman down the street with tattoos on her knuckles gives us recipes for significant wounds. We have denied ourselves care—forever ready for the trauma. She cranks out a tincture and we can smell it from our house. We have rats in the lurking place. We're told to poison the water, put out fruit jar traps. Divert a stream. Keep our matches and fuzz sticks dry. We try to reduce the effects of their damage.

Pilot Plants

wild leek / pigweed / solomon's seal / fireweed / thistle / trembling aspen / pawpaw / curly dock / lamb's quarter / honey mesquite / wild rose /pigweed / gooseberry / sweetgale / field pennycress / yellow pond lily / arrowhead / burdock / cattail / chickweed / miner's lettuce / sheep sorrel / white mustard / pasture brake

Throw Ring

Orange is a vest for hunting, the ring for saving at sea. Our mother's hands are gone from where they held applause. Her orange lips bringing a note in her throat. Her fingernails are circus peanuts. Her hands, sunrays, we sunned ourselves in. We line the windowsills with tangerines. Her mouth—a warning that she would be found if she wanted to be saved.

Levels of Force

They took a part of her from us, and we put sea stars on her wounds. We sing at each other and wear day lily chains. We forfeit. Vines squeeze the house in and we let them. We think they will grow over the door and run up to the sky. The school buses here are stunned fish, abandoned in the woods—vases for ivy that finds them. Like a folk tale, we'll climb up and find our parents there the whole time.

There's a Gap in the Land

Cows line the rim of a pond and they will survive the heat. We don't sleep under dead trees. We treat emergency injuries as soon as we see them. There's a gap in the land and it's where we want to hide. We want to cover this whole town up, with their cow patties and cow tipping and toilet paper rolling. They leave markers where people die if it happened on a road. We want our parents to arrive breathing in their mouths saying *we just wanted to know that you would be okay without us.*

Root Division

The father is a bridge. You have to move toward something always. You have to use the bud and the stem. You have to stand at a threshold and know that it's going to be a meadow. What happens when you lose two bridges? We become the bridge. We're the judge and the jury and the click beetles digging until we find our parents back, their shadows rising over what we make and unmake in the sand.

Outlines

We wear chains of bear bells around our waists and wade into foxfire. Watch. We are sailors glowing in pilot lights. We pick valerian that sings us to bed before atlases beat themselves against the glass that doesn't belong to them but to the sinking house. Their migration surrounds, and we come out with our hands open, grabbing at nothing. And, when this house drowns, we'll be failed sailors. Our outlines in foxfire, burning until a star mutes them.

In Case of Abduction

6/1	flags tank	striped shirt
	camouflage pants	stars leggings
	blaze orange vest	blaze orange vest
6/2	flags tank	alligator shirt
	horse shorts	plaid shorts
	blaze orange vest	blaze orange vest
6/3	alligator shirt	black dot shirt
	horse shorts	camouflage pants
	blaze orange vest	blaze orange vest
6/4	striped shirt	paint sweatshirt
	plaid shorts	stars leggings
	blaze orange vest	blaze orange vest
6/5	flags tank	alligator shirt
	ripped stirrups	camouflage pants
	blaze orange vest	blaze orange vest
6/6	paint sweatshirt	flags tank
	horse shorts	stars leggings
	blaze orange vest	blaze orange vest
6/7	striped shirt	black dot shirt
	camouflage pants	plaid shorts
	blaze orange vest	blaze orange vest
6/8	paint sweatshirt	alligator shirt
	camouflage pants	plaid shorts
	blaze orange vest	blaze orange vest
6/9	paint sweatshirt	striped shirt
	camouflage pants	stars leggings
	blaze orange vest	

6/10	paint sweatshirt	black dot shirt
	camouflage pants	horse shorts
6/11		
6/12		
6/13		
6/14		
6/15		
6/16		

An Emotional Memory

How many crickets chirp make one degree? Home, we'd watch fish jump on the top of the water for rain. Here, we translate the leaves' turns like our father's face when he stirred his brush in a stripped spinach can. Our mother smelled like raw silk all year. Even after eating lemon wedge after wedge. Our father called her sea moth. We can't smell her here. It smells like moss and wood and moon. We've become even more animal. We use our snouts to carry the berry buckets, to find our way back.

Land Survey

When the first storm of our lives came to us, we asked our father, *What if it kills us?* His face, a static triangle, *Today isn't the day we die.* Now we watch branches drop in our front yard like poured walls. Our street is a line of branches cleaved by weather. Water collected during disaster is more charged. We won't buck the tree until the leaves are poised, brown, dead and can't hold nests and live birds.

Made in the Woods

Floating logs ignite, burn. All the fury is finally here. Trees hurl and burn quickly. A set of bones once moved here. Not a fire spilling lost, racing down, not fast enough. Bodies in positions of flight. One wife who played cards alone fought a burning house by hand. Darkness remembered the name of fire as a child. One forest rolled with lights, coughing their way toward smoke. A suffocated cave, smoke robbing the dark. Eventually, wind rolled into rain. The fire, the one after the last, died out.

Send a Revival

We walk into open woods at night, ready for the palm to finally shut our crying up. We're looking for a bear who can't see us and can't hear us now. If we were home, we would swim noiseless out past the warnings. We'd say here's the rip that sweeps our bodies under and into her chest. This is where we were born. This is where we became orphans, where we stayed on top of the water. This is where we say no more.

Acknowledgments

I am very grateful to the editors of the following journals where these poems first appeared, at times as earlier versions.

$: "Topographies," "Low Recitation" and "The Start of the Thread"
Avoid Disaster: "Glory Pact"
Cream City Review: "Outlines"
Journal of Compressed Creative Arts: "Field Test"
PANK: "Made in the Woods"
Puerto del Sol: "Affirmations" and "Tragedy Lessons"
The Indianapolis Review: "Half a Parade" and "Here, in the Summer"
The Rupture: "Beginnings of Nature" and "Dear Outsiders"

Thank you always to my mermaid mom who talked with me about beach towns and her watery memories. Thank you to my dad and his mountains, who encouraged me to write about my fears. Stephanie, you're here in every page.

Enormous gratitude to the most generous advocate for poets and poetry, Mary Biddinger. Thank you for seeing this manuscript and for your incredible support and care. I want to thank Jon and Thea and everyone at the University of Akron Press for making me feel so welcome. I'm grateful for the immensely talented Cristina Daura whose illustration truly captures the world of the book. Thank you to Amy Freels for the stunning cover design. Endless thanks to Erika Meitner.

Thank you to Komal for all of it. Rebecca, thank you for being a first reader of these poems so long ago.

Jennifer, I cannot thank you enough for holding and guiding these poems and all the poems over the years. Thank you to Cynthia for our talks and for your incredible notes. To Traci for keeping me accountable.

Thank you to Alison C. Rollins, Jessica Q. Stark, and Vanessa Angélica Villarreal, for your stunning work that I go back to again and again and for your support.

Thank you to the Hambidge Center for giving me the space to write these poems and for the bell.

Who would I be without my teachers. Who would I be without my students.

Nate, for going on adventures with me and for propping me up. For being my anchor.

Bella, you're my whole heart.

Jenny Sadre-Orafai is an Iranian Mexican American poet and writer. She is the coauthor of *Book of Levitations* and the author of *Malak* and *Paper, Cotton, Leather.* Her poetry has appeared in *Cream City Review, Ninth Letter, The Cortland Review,* and *Hotel Amerika.* Her prose has appeared in *VIDA Review, Fourteen Hills,* and *The Los Angeles Review.* She co-founded *Josephine Quarterly* and teaches creative writing at Kennesaw State University.